HE LIVES

Music and Lyrics by Hilary Weeks

Artwork by Simon Dewey

DESERET
BOOK

SALT LAKE CITY, UTAH

Text and Lyrics © 2004 Hilary Weeks

Text and Illustrations © 2004 Simon Dewey

Visit us at deseretbook.com

Library of Congress Cataloging-in-Publication Data
Weeks, Hilary.
  He lives / Hilary Weeks, [illustrated by] Simon Dewey.
    p.   cm.
  ISBN-10 1-59038-270-6 (hard : alk. paper)
  ISBN-13 978-1-59038-270-7 (hard : alk. paper)
  1. Contemporary Christian music—Texts.   2. Jesus Christ—Songs and music.
3. Jesus Christ—Art.   I. Dewey, Simon.   II. Title.
  ML54.6.W24 2004
  782.27'0268—dc22   2003025391

Printed in Mexico
R. R. Donnelley, Reynosa, Mexico

10 9 8 7 6

To all who seek the Savior:

May you come to know Him

better through the artwork and

music that are testimonies of Him.

—HILARY WEEKS AND SIMON DEWEY

"My Brother, My Savior, My Friend" inspires me to be grateful for all Jesus Christ has done, continues to do, and will do for me in times to come. Perhaps the most influential moment in the song is when Hilary, with a rising crescendo, declares triumphantly, "He lives. I know He lives." I think the reason this song is so moving is because it reveals to me a Jesus that is powerful enough to save a world from death but personal enough to love a sinner, such as I, with a love that never ends. The Messiah, who changed the world forever, is also our humble friend. —SIMON DEWEY

MY BROTHER, MY SAVIOR, MY FRIEND

He touched the blind,
and they were made to see.

And through His love,
He heals you and me.

He is a friend to the man
without a home, and
He's our shelter in the storm.

Simon Dewey

And he will take upon him death, that he may loose the bands of death which bind his people; and

he will take upon him their infirmities, that his bowels may be filled with mercy, according to the flesh,

that he may know according to the flesh how to succor his people according to their infirmities.

—Alma 7:12

He broke the chains that bound me and you

And set us free by unlocking the truth.

He paid the price, knowing death would be the cost,

Saving souls that would be lost.

And I believe

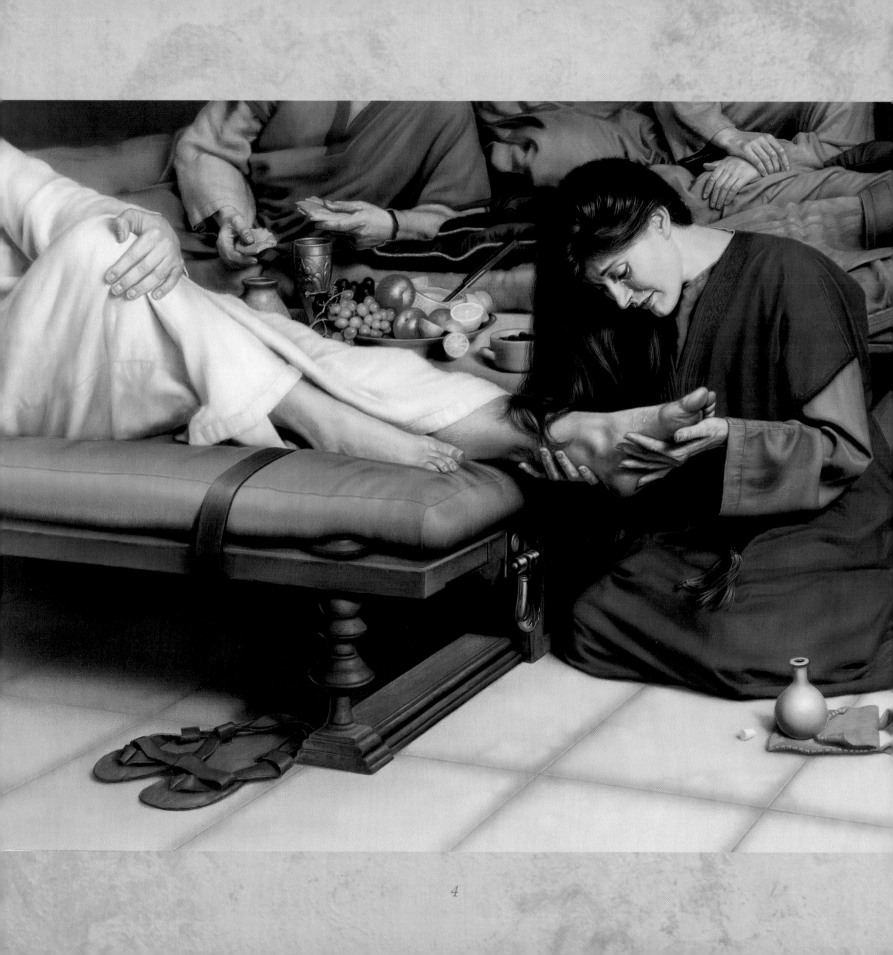

Simon Dewey

That He lives.

I know He lives.

And everyday He's watching over me.

And His great love will never end

For He's my Brother, my Savior, my Friend.

And when I think of all He's done for me,

I want to live so that someday I'll kneel at His feet

And I'll thank Him with my tears for His love
through the years, and I will see

I am the resurrection, and the life: he that believeth in me,

though he were dead, yet shall he live.

—John 11:25

That He lives.

> *Yes, He lives.*

And everyday He's watching over me.

> *And with His love I cannot fall,*

For He's my Brother, my Savior, my all,

> *The One I turn to who'll always understand,*
>
> *The One who gave His life so we could live again.*

And His great love will never end,

> *For He's our Brother, our Savior, our Friend.*

Simon Dewey

Have ye any that are sick among you? Bring them hither. Have ye any that are lame, or blind,

or halt, or maimed, or leprous, or that are withered, or that are deaf, or that are afflicted in any manner?

Bring them hither and I will heal them, for I have compassion upon you; my bowels are filled with mercy.

—3 Nephi 17:7

GREATER MIRACLES

Have you any that are sick? Bring them here, He will heal them.

Have you any that are lame, bent in pain, hurt, or yearning?

Bring them all—old and young—and He will lift them up.

He will make them whole, and if they put their faith in Him,
they shall see greater miracles than these.

Have you children who are blind?

      Bring them here, He will bless them.

He will truly make them see wondrous things

      when you let them

go to Him on bended knee, and He will lift them up.

      He will make them whole.

And if they put their faith in Him,

      they shall see greater miracles than these.

Simon Dewey

I love Simon's artwork. I am amazed at his ability to tell a story with the stroke of a brush and at his gift for capturing immense emotion in the faces of those he paints. Most of all, I appreciate the feelings of love, gratitude, and reverence I feel for the Savior when I look at Simon's paintings.

In "Arise and Walk," my eyes go first to the young mother. Placed in circumstances beyond her control, the course of her life changed. Unwilling to leave her small child, she is left to sit in the street, small bowl by her side, begging for assistance.

At the mercy of any who will give, she cradles her small son in her lap. A man approaches. Sensing her son's hesitation, she wraps her hand around his tiny fist. She knows the man who now stands before them offers more than temporal gifts—a second chance, the ability to rise above weaknesses and walk with Him. She understands the Savior's power.

Simon captures all that is good about mothers: faith, gratitude, gentleness, unconditional love, patience.

There have been many times in my life when I have reached out for the Savior's hand. At those moments, He has healed my imperfections, my shortcomings, my heart. He has lifted me. I am grateful for the miracles I have experienced in my life. —HILARY WEEKS

Did you know that He can heal the widow's broken heart?

That His love can change your life, save a world torn apart?

Did you know that He holds the earth and sky at His command?

But when you feel forgiveness come, then you'll understand,

That's the miracle . . . the greatest miracle.

Do your burdens weigh you down?

> *Go to Him, He will lift them.*

As your brother, as your friend,

> *He has love enough for all men.*

Trust in Him, take His hand,

And He will lift you up, He will make you whole.

And if you put your faith in Him,

> *you shall see greater miracles than these,*

Greater miracles than these.

Simon Dewey

Simon Dewey

ALL MY DAYS

Love and grace brought Him here,

A world to save, He suffered all.

    He felt our pain. He knew it was the only way.

He understands when I'm unsure. He knows the plan.

And when I'm tired, losing my way,

    He picks me up and gives me strength.

And I will praise Him

As the Savior stands in the archway to this home, he emulates strength. He looks sure, true, and confident. The doves, symbols of peace, know the Savior's gentle and kind nature and are not afraid. In fact, they are coming to Him, even flying towards His outstretched hand.

The glow in the window and doorway intrigue me. Don't we all wish the Savior stood in the doorway of our homes, illuminating the walls, windows, and stairways with light only He can bring? I too feel the Savior's light in our home when we have invited Him in. Perhaps there is no door in this painting, simply an archway, to remind us to never close our hearts to Him. May we continually invite our Savior, the Prince of Peace, into our hearts and homes that His light and peace might dwell therein. —HILARY WEEKS

I will praise thee, O Lord, with my whole heart;

I will shew forth all thy marvellous works.

—PSALM 9:1

All my days,

All my days.

May my voice ring out in praise

For Him who died

To give me life.

I will glory in His name

All my days.

19

Simon Dewey

O Lord, thou art my God; I will exalt thee, I will praise thy name; for thou hast done wonderful things; thy counsels of old are faithfulness and truth.

—Isaiah 25:1

He sends His love so patiently.

He teaches me step by step,

Leading me home.

It's the greatest love I've ever known,

And I will praise Him

All my days.

May my voice ring out in praise

For Him who died

To give me life.

I will glory in His name

All my days.

In the song "When He Calls My Name," Hilary has managed to capture a portion of my personal testimony and made it tender and beautiful with music. That is the power of the medium in which she works and is the reason why I never paint without the CD player on. I am grateful for the little bit of light and understanding that has been allotted to me, which tells me that in some future day, if I am worthy, I will be permitted to praise in person the Divine Redeemer Himself. I know that I will require His mercy, but to hear Him utter the words, "Well done, thou good and faithful servant," would be the crowning achievement of my life. —SIMON DEWEY

For the time is at hand; the day or the hour no man knoweth; but it surely shall come. And he that receiveth these things receiveth me; and they shall be gathered unto me in time and in eternity.

—D&C 39:21–22

WHEN HE CALLS MY NAME

The hour is drawing closer,
though no man knows the day

When He'll come in all His glory
and we'll meet Him face to face.

I will marvel at His goodness,
and my voice will shout His praise

As I rise to meet the Savior
when He calls my name.

Simon Dewey

Simon Dewey

The Lord hath redeemed my soul from hell; I have beheld his glory,

and I am encircled about eternally in the arms of his love.

—2 Nephi 1:15

I will bow before His glory as the tears freely flow.

Though I won't have words to tell Him all I'm feeling,

I hope He'll know I've waited for this day

And His embrace.

I'll come running when He calls my name.

Search me, O God, and know my heart: try me, and know my thoughts.

—Psalm 139:23

I will look to Him for mercy as He looks into my heart.

How I long to be found worthy to have
Him smile and say, "Well done"

When He reaches out His hands,
and I touch them and I feel them.

With my eyes no longer closed,
when I see that He died for me

I will bow before His glory as the tears freely flow.

Though I won't have words to tell Him all I'm feeling,
I hope He'll know I've lived for this day

To praise His name.
I'll embrace Him when He calls my name.

Simon Dewey

Simon Dewey

I am the light and the life of the world.

I am Alpha and Omega,

the beginning and the end.

—3 NEPHI 9:18

H E I S

He is the first ray of sun to reach above the mountain.

He is a gentle ocean breeze on my face.

He is raindrops moving slowly down my window.

He is a long deep breath at the end of the day.

I grew up in Anchorage, Alaska, where nature's grandeur is breathtaking. I would often walk to a particularly beautiful spot near my home where I could sit in the forest while gazing at the ocean and mountains. It was the perfect setting for quiet moments to ponder and pray.

I have always found solitude and a sense of clarity in the midst of the Savior's creations. For me, it is easy to see the Creator through His creations. I find Him in the simple things— good deeds, kind words, raindrops. Everything witnesses of the Savior, Jesus Christ. Whether it is the simple beauties of the Earth or the magnitude of His Atonement, the gifts He offers touch the lives of each of us.

I know He lives. I feel His hand in my life as He guides me on the pathway home. He is my constant source of strength. He is my Redeemer. He is everything. —HILARY WEEKS

Behold, I am Jesus Christ the Son of God. I created the

heavens and the earth, and all things that in them are.

—3 Nephi 9:15

He is a warm afternoon at the end of September.

He is a brilliant sunset sky.

He is a silent snowfall and the deafening crash of thunder.

He is endless stars on a cloudless night.

Simon Dewey

32

And whoso shall receive one such

little child in my name receiveth me.

—Matthew 18:5

He is the laughter of children

And the wonder in their eyes.

On a distant rocky shore,

He's a clear and steady light.

Simon Dewey

*He is wrinkled hands
and tiny
newborn fingers.*

*He is the beckon that
calls you home.*

*He is the sturdy staff
that leads you
to drink beside
still waters.*

*He is the reason why
the lilies grow.*

And I will bring the blind by a way that they knew not;

I will lead them in paths that they have not known: I will

make darkness light before them, and crooked things straight.

These things will I do unto them, and not forsake them.

—Isaiah 42:16

He is a sermon on a mount.

He is a widow and her mite.

He is the blind man's first glimpse of light.

He is a garden and a prayer.

He is two strangers on a hill.

He is an empty tomb

And the price that heaven paid.

He's our chance to try again.

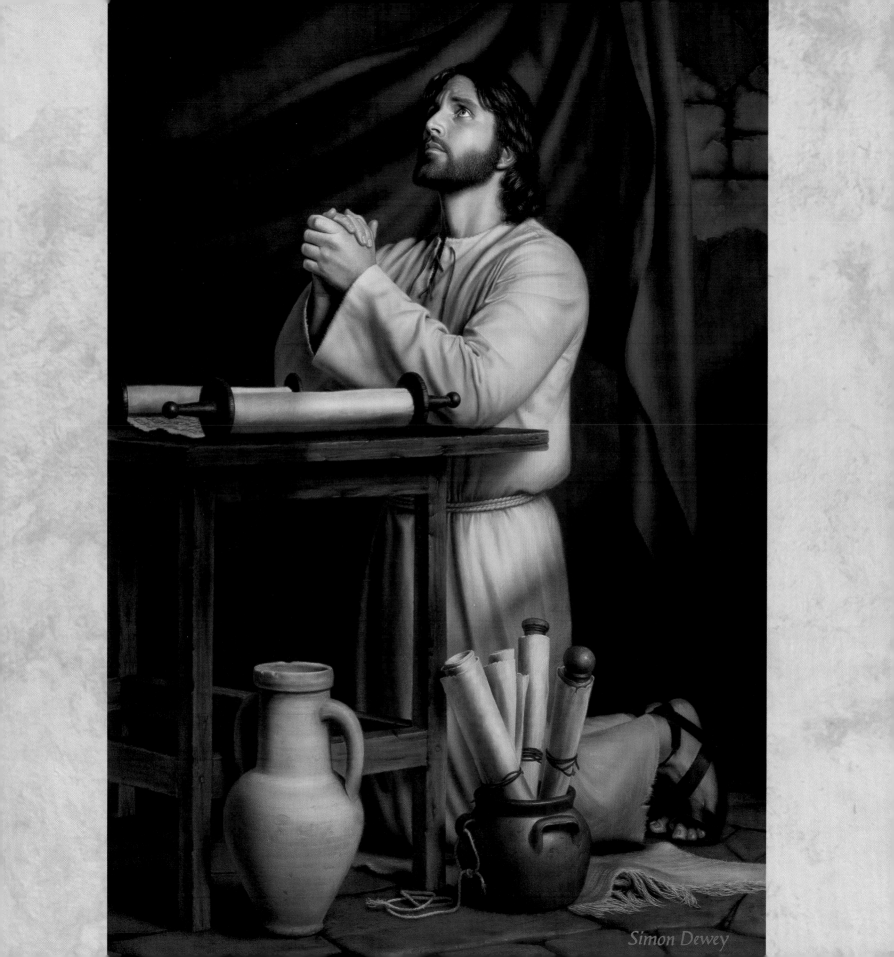

I am the way, the truth, and the life:

no man cometh unto the Father, but by me.

—JOHN 14:6

He is open arms.

He is a quiet invitation.

He is hope when hope is gone.

He is lasting peace and the
answer we are seeking.

He is the pathway home.

He is.

Yes, He is.

Simon Dewey

ILLUSTRATION CREDITS

1	FROM DARKNESS TO LIGHT
2	BEHOLD THE MAN
4–5	FOR SHE LOVED MUCH
7	HE LIVES
8	DAUGHTER, ARISE
11	CONSIDER THE LILIES
12	ARISE AND WALK
15	IN HUMILITY
16	O MY FATHER
19	PRINCE OF PEACE
20	LIGHT AND TRUTH
23	LIVING WATER
24	TOUCH OF FAITH
27	WHY WEEPEST THOU?
28	FISHERS OF MEN
31	THE LORD IS MY SHEPHERD
32	OF SUCH IS THE KINGDOM
34	MY SON, MY SAVIOR
35	BESIDE STILL WATERS
36	HEAR YE HIM
38	THE LAST SUPPER
39	HALLOWED BE THY NAME
41	DIVINE REDEEMER

SONG CREDITS